Yellow Umbrella Books are published by Red Brick Learning
151 Good Counsel Drive, P.O. Box 669, Mankato, Minnesota 56002
www.redbricklearning.com

*Library of Congress Cataloging-in-Publication Data*
Trumbauer, Lisa, 1963–
  Why we measure / by Lisa Trumbauer.
    p. cm.—(Math)
    Includes Index.
  Summary: Explains that people take measurements to find out how tall, how long, how far, how fast, how heavy, how much, and what size.
  ISBN 0-7368-2017-5 (hardcover)
  1. Mensuration—Juvenile literature. [1. Measurement.] I. Title. II. Series.
  QA465.T78 2003
  530.8—dc21
                                                                    2003000934

**Editorial Credits**
Mary Lindeen, Editorial Director; Jennifer Van Voorst, Editor; Wanda Winch, Photo Researcher

**Photo Credits**
Cover: Rob Van Petten/DigitalVision; Title Page: PhotoLink/PhotoDisc; Page 2: Creatas; Page 3 - Page 5: Jim Foell/Capstone Press; Page 6: Creatas; Page 7: Joseph Sohm/ ChromoSohm, Inc./Corbis; Page 8: PhotoLink/PhotoDisc; Page 9: PhotoLink/PhotoDisc; Page 10: D. Berry/PhotoLink/PhotoDisc; Page 11: Stockbyte; Page 12: Jim Foell/Capstone Press; Page 13: Phil Bulgasch/Capstone Press; Page 14 - Page 16: Jim Foell/Capstone Press

1 2 3 4 5 6 08 07 06 05 04 03

# Why We Measure

by Lisa Trumbauer

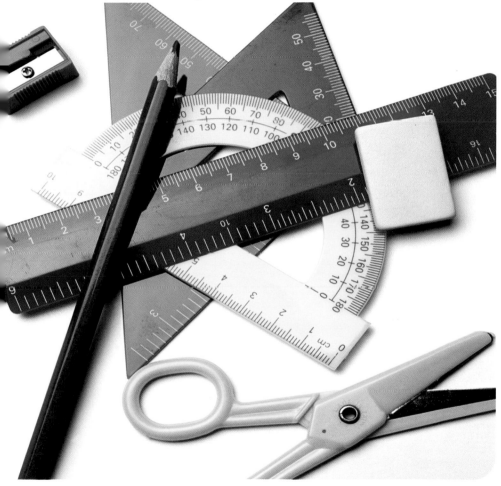

Consultants: David Olson, Director of Undergraduate Studies, and
Tamara Olson, Associate Professor, Department of Mathematical Sciences,
Michigan Technological University

Yellow Umbrella Books
an imprint of Red Brick Learning
Mankato, Minnesota

# We measure to find out how tall.

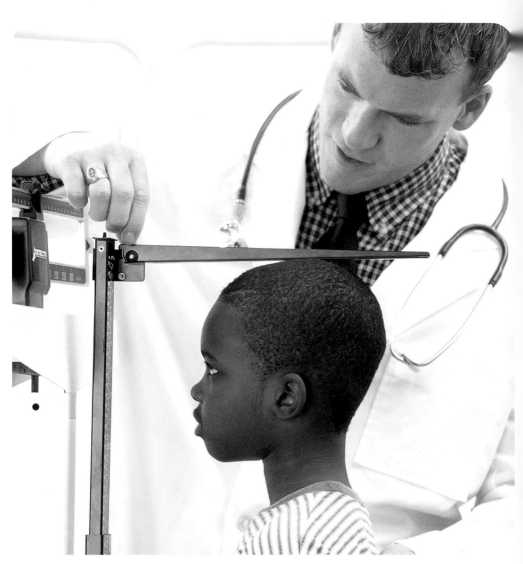

# This tells us how tall.

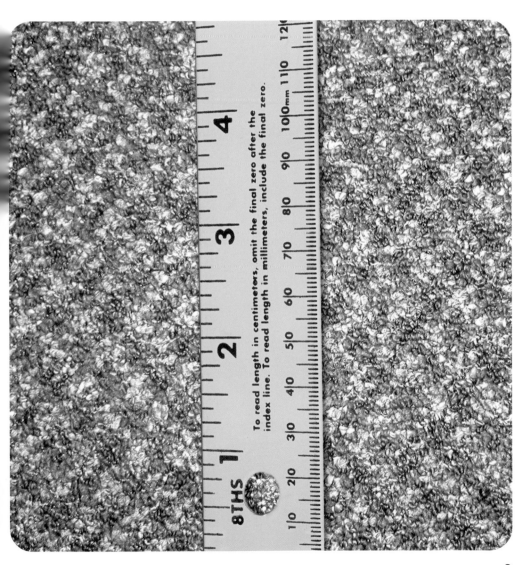

# We measure to find out how long.

# This tells us how long.

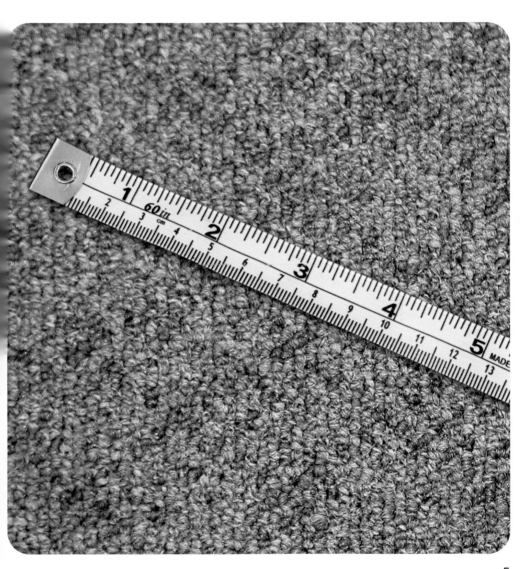

# We measure to find out how far.

# This tells us how far.

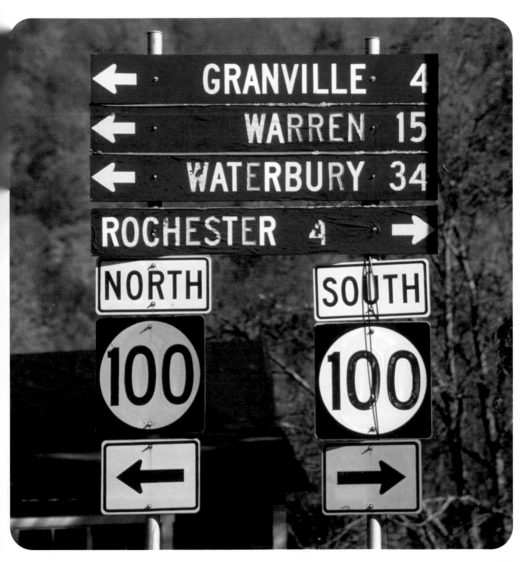

# We measure to find out how fast.

# This tells us how fast.

# We measure to find out how heavy.

# This tells us how heavy.

# We measure to find out how much.

# This tells us how much.

# We measure to find out what size.

# This tells us what size.

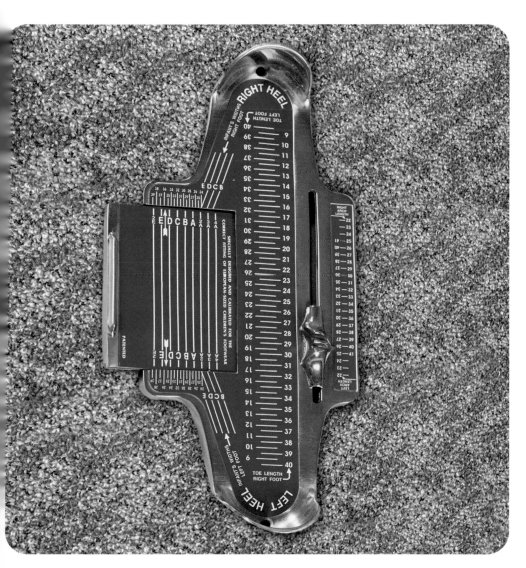

# What do you measure?

# Words to Know/Index

Word Count: 88
Early-Intervention Level: 7